IT'S TIME TO EAT
RED CABBAGE

It's Time to Eat RED CABBAGE

Walter the Educator

Silent King Books
A WhichHead Entertainment Imprint

Copyright © 2024 by Walter the Educator

All rights reserved. No part of this book may be reproduced in any manner whatsoever without written per- mission except in the case of brief quotations embodied in critical articles and reviews.

First Printing, 2024

Disclaimer

This book is a literary work; the story is not about specific persons, locations, situations, and/or circumstances unless mentioned in a historical context. Any resemblance to real persons, locations, situations, and/or circumstances is coincidental. This book is for entertainment and informational purposes only. The author and publisher offer this information without warranties expressed or implied. No matter the grounds, neither the author nor the publisher will be accountable for any losses, injuries, or other damages caused by the reader's use of this book. The use of this book acknowledges an understanding and acceptance of this disclaimer.

It's Time to Eat RED CABBAGE is a collectible early learning book by Walter the Educator suitable for all ages belonging to Walter the Educator's Time to Eat Book Series. Collect more books at WaltertheEducator.com

USE THE EXTRA SPACE TO TAKE NOTES AND DOCUMENT YOUR MEMORIES

RED CABBAGE

It's time to eat, come take a peek,

It's Time to Eat

Red Cabbage

Red cabbage is the star this week!

With purple leaves that shine so bright,

It's crunchy, tasty, and just right.

Round and snug, it grows so tight,

A veggie ball that's quite the sight.

Slice it up and watch it gleam,

Red cabbage adds a purple dream!

In salads raw, it's fresh and sweet,

A colorful crunch that can't be beat.

Or cook it soft, so warm and nice,

Red cabbage pairs with every slice.

It's full of power, did you know?

Vitamins to help you grow!

Each purple bite is oh so smart,

It keeps your brain and body in heart.

It's Time to Eat

Red Cabbage

Imagine it's a flower's bloom,

Bright and bold to fill your room.

Or a purple crown for your veggie king,

On your plate, it's everything!

Chop, chop, chop, it's fun to do,

Watch the colors change for you!

A splash of vinegar, a dash of spice,

Turns red cabbage into something nice.

In tacos, soups, or roasted slow,

Red cabbage makes your meals just glow.

It's fun to eat and fun to see,

A veggie treat for you and me!

Crunchy, crispy, or silky and sweet,

Red cabbage is always a joy to eat.

It's Time to Eat

Red Cabbage

It helps you jump, it helps you run,

A veggie so cool, it's always fun!

Take a bite, don't wait too long,

Red cabbage will make you strong.

With every munch, you'll surely see,

It's packed with love and energy.

Thank you, cabbage, round and red,

For filling our bellies and being well-fed.

We love your color, your crunch, your cheer,

It's Time to Eat

Red Cabbage

Red cabbage, you're the veggie of the year!

ABOUT THE CREATOR

Walter the Educator is one of the pseudonyms for Walter Anderson. Formally educated in Chemistry, Business, and Education, he is an educator, an author, a diverse entrepreneur, and he is the son of a disabled war veteran. "Walter the Educator" shares his time between educating and creating. He holds interests and owns several creative projects that entertain, enlighten, enhance, and educate, hoping to inspire and motivate you. Follow, find new works, and stay up to date with Walter the Educator™ at WaltertheEducator.com

www.ingramcontent.com/pod-product-compliance
Lightning Source LLC
LaVergne TN
LVHW052014060526
838201LV00059B/4031